UEFA EURO 2016 FRANCE

FACT FILE

Clive Gifford

CARLTON KiDS

CONTENTS

Note to reader: the facts and records in this book are accurate as of 30 January 2016.

CHAMPIONS AND HOSTS

There have been 14 editions of the UEFA European Football Championship and now the focus turns to France for EURO 2016. The tournaments have been held all over Europe, and the number of teams contesting the finals has steadily risen.

1960
HOSTS: France
TEAMS: Four
FINAL: Soviet Union 2-1 Yugoslavia (after extra time)
VENUE: Parc des Princes, Paris

In this, the first ever tournament, Yugoslavia came back from two goals down to beat France 5-4 and reach the final, where they were narrowly beaten by the Soviet Union.

1964

HOSTS: Spain
TEAMS: Four
FINAL: Spain 2-1 Soviet Union
VENUE: Estadio Santiago Bernabéu, Madrid

With Hungary and Denmark knocked out, Spain faced holders the Soviet Union for the trophy. Jesús María Pereda's sixth-minute goal for Spain remains the fastest scored in a EURO final.

1968
HOSTS: Italy
TEAMS: Four
FINAL: Italy 2-0 Yugoslavia
VENUE: Stadio Olimpico, Rome

Debutants Italy won a coin toss to progress to the final after drawing 0-0 with the Soviet Union. After a 1-1 draw, the final was replayed two days later and the Italians triumphed.

1972
HOSTS: Belgium
TEAMS: Four
FINAL: West Germany 3-0 Soviet Union
VENUE: Heysel Stadium, Brussels

West Germany eased past Belgium in the semi-final and then beat the Soviet Union in front of 43,437 fans. Gerd Müller was the tournament's top-scorer, with two goals in each of the two games.

1976
HOSTS: Yugoslavia
TEAMS: Four
FINAL: Czechoslovakia 2-2 West Germany (5-3 pens)
VENUE: Red Star Stadium, Belgrade

The Netherlands made their tournament debut, finishing third, and the final was the first to go to a penalty shoot-out. Antonín Panenka's audacious chipped penalty gave Czechoslovakia their first major football trophy.

1980
HOSTS: Italy
TEAMS: Eight
FINAL: West Germany 2-1 Belgium
VENUE: Stadio Olimpico, Rome

In an expanded eight-team competition, the hosts qualified automatically for the first time. West Germany triumphed and provided six of the 11 players in the UEFA Team of the Tournament. Italy won the last ever EURO third-place play-off, defeating Czechoslovakia on penalties.

1984
HOSTS: France
TEAMS: Eight
FINAL: France 2-0 Spain
VENUE: Parc des Princes, Paris

Hosts France won for the first time, with Michel Platini the undoubted star of the competition. He scored nine goals and remains the only player to score two hat-tricks in one finals tournament.

Gothenburg 1992
London 1996
Rotterdam 2000
Brussels 1972
Paris 1960 & 1984
Munich 1988
Vienna 2008
Madrid 1964
Lisbon 2004
Belgrade 1976
Rome 1968 & 1980

1988

HOSTS: West Germany
TEAMS: Eight
FINAL: Netherlands 2-0 Soviet Union
VENUE: Olympiastadion, Munich

The Netherlands knocked the hosts out at the semi-final stage and won the competition for the first time. Tournament top-scorer Marco van Basten's fifth goal was a stunning volley in the final.

1992

HOSTS: Sweden
TEAMS: Eight
FINAL: Denmark 2-0 Germany
VENUE: Ullevi, Gothenberg

Denmark replaced Yugoslavia at the last minute and despite their lack of preparation, Brian Laudrup and Peter Schmeichel helped the team past France, the Netherlands and a unified Germany to become surprise champions.

1996

HOSTS: England
TEAMS: Sixteen
FINAL: Germany 2-1 Czech Republic
VENUE: Wembley Stadium, London

Over 1.27 million people flocked to the first 16-team tournament. England reached the semi-finals, with Alan Shearer the tournament's top-scorer, but Germany lifted the trophy thanks to Oliver Bierhoff scoring the EUROs' first-ever golden goal.

2000

HOSTS: Belgium, the Netherlands
TEAMS: Sixteen
FINAL: France 2-1 Italy
VENUE: Stadion Feijenoord, Rotterdam

In the first co-hosted tournament, Group A saw Portugal and Romania qualify at the expense of Germany and England, while Zinedine Zidane's France became the first FIFA World Cup holders to win the competition.

2004

HOSTS: Portugal
TEAMS: Sixteen
FINAL: Greece 1-0 Portugal
VENUE: Estádio da Luz, Lisbon

This tournament of shocks saw Italy, Spain and Germany failing to get out of their groups. That was topped however by Greece, playing in only their second EURO finals tournament, becoming unlikely champions.

Kyiv 2012

2008

HOSTS: Austria, Switzerland
TEAMS: Sixteen
FINAL: Spain 1-0 Germany
VENUE: Ernst-Happel-Stadion, Vienna

Spain's David Villa was the tournament's top-scorer, with four goals, but his team-mate Fernando Torres scored the winner in the final. Spain also registered their first competitive win against Italy in 88 years.

2012

HOSTS: Poland, Ukraine
TEAMS: Sixteen
FINAL: Spain 4-0 Italy
VENUE: Olympic Stadium, Kyiv

More than 1.44 million fans enjoyed a tournament that featured 76 goals and six joint top-scorers. Spain, propelled by Andrés Iniesta, became the first team to win the competition twice in a row.

THE ROAD TO EURO 2016

The quest to reach France and EURO 2016 began on 7 September 2014 with the first round of qualification matches. Fifty-three nations entered qualifying, each aiming to win one of the 23 places at the finals tournament alongside the hosts, France. The teams included Gibraltar, who were taking part for the first time but suffered three 7-0 defeats, as well as an 8-1 thrashing by Poland. In all, 694 goals were scored from 6,543 attempts on goal during qualifying. There were surprises in store with regular EURO competitors such as the Netherlands (champions in 1988), Greece (the winners in 2004) and Bulgaria all missing out, while Albania, Northern Ireland, Slovakia and Iceland reached the finals for the first time.

WELCOME TO FRANCE

In 2016, France will host the UEFA European Football Championship finals for the third time in the tournament's history. The country, with its rich history, culture and food, its beautiful countryside and spectacular cities, is one of the most visited nations on the planet. Around 2.5 million fans, more than in any previous tournament, are expected to attend EURO 2016. At each of the host cities there will be entertainment and dedicated fan zones, each of which will provide a fun football atmosphere with giant screens displaying live match action.

Super Victor is the official mascot of EURO 2016. His name was chosen by public vote.

French fans fly the flag for their team during warm-up games for EURO 2016.

With home support, the French will hope to progress well beyond the group stages.

THE TROPHY

Henri Delaunay (1883-1955) was a French footballer and the first UEFA general secretary. He pioneered the idea of a European-wide football competition. His son Pierre oversaw the design of the trophy for the first tournament in 1960. It was replaced for EURO 2008 by a heavier, larger version of the original – 60cm tall, weighing 8kg and made of sterling silver.

© UEFA 2006

Michel Platini (*centre left*) scored 41 goals for France and became UEFA president in 2007.

INTERNATIONAL CHAMPIONS

France has a long and illustrious footballing history. *Les Bleus* have finished in the top four at five FIFA World Cups, were world champions in 1998 and won the UEFA European Football Championship in 1984 and 2000. France have won the FIFA Confederations Cup twice (2001, 2003) and were Olympic champions in 1984.

TOP TEAMS AND PLAYERS

FIFA, world football's governing body, was formed in Paris in 1904, while UEFA's first headquarters and its first general secretary were both French. French clubs, including Olympique de Marseille, Paris Saint-Germain and AS Saint-Étienne, have made it to the final of 13 European competitions, including the UEFA Champions League. Famous players such as Just Fontaine, Michel Platini, Zinedine Zidane, Thierry Henry and Franck Ribéry have graced the game at both club and national level, roared on by France's passionate fans.

THE VENUES

The 51 matches of EURO 2016 will be played in ten cities across France. The final will be staged in the Stade de France in Saint-Denis.

STADE DE FRANCE
HOST CITY: Saint-Denis
CAPACITY: 80,000
STADIUM FACT: The opening match and the final take place in France's national stadium, located in Saint-Denis to the north of Paris. It is the sixth-largest stadium in Europe.

STADE PIERRE MAUROY
HOST CITY: Lille
CAPACITY: 50,000
STADIUM FACT: Home to the Ligue 1 club LOSC Lille. Rated five stars by UEFA, this multi-use stadium will host group games and one of the quarter-finals.

STADE BOLLAERT-DELELIS
HOST CITY: Lens
CAPACITY: 38,000
STADIUM FACT: Home to RC Lens (short for Racing Club of Lens), it was one of the venues for the 1998 FIFA World Cup and has been upgraded for EURO 2016.

PARC DES PRINCES
HOST CITY: Paris
CAPACITY: 48,000
STADIUM FACT: This all-seater venue has been home to Paris Saint-Germain since 1973. It was the original national stadium of the French team and has been redeveloped for EURO 2016.

STADE DE LYON
HOST CITY: Lyon
CAPACITY: 59,000
STADIUM FACT: This brand-new stadium, built by the French Ligue 1 club Olympique Lyonnais, will host one of the semi-finals.

LILLE

LENS

SAINT-DENIS

PARIS

STADE DE NICE

HOST CITY: Nice
CAPACITY: 36,000
STADIUM FACT: This eco-friendly new arena opened in 2013 and is the home of OGC Nice. Over 4,000 solar panels generate more than three times the energy required to run the stadium.

Map labels:

- NICE
- MARSEILLE
- LYON
- SAINT-ÉTIENNE
- TOULOUSE
- BORDEAUX

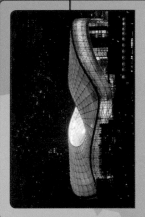

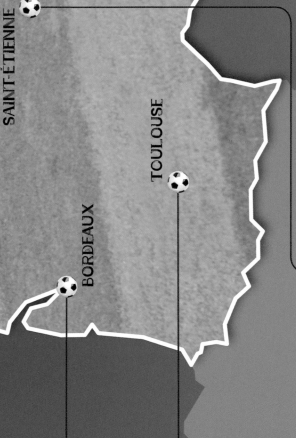

STADE VÉLODROME

HOST CITY: Marseille
CAPACITY: 67,000
STADIUM FACT: Originally built for the 1938 FIFA World Cup and home to Olympique de Marseille, the redeveloped stadium will host a quarter-final and a semi-final.

STADE GEOFFROY GUICHARD

HOST CITY: Saint-Étienne
CAPACITY: 42,000
STADIUM FACT: The first stadium opened in 1931 and had just 800 seats. Following many expansions over the years, it has been redeveloped for EURO 2016.

STADE DE BORDEAUX

HOST CITY: Bordeaux
CAPACITY: 42,000
STADIUM FACT: This brand-new stadium is the home of Ligue 1 club FC Girondins de Bordeaux and will host one of the quarter-finals.

STADIUM DE TOULOUSE

HOST CITY: Toulouse
CAPACITY: 33,000
STADIUM FACT: The smallest of the ten venues, it hosted FIFA World Cup matches in 1938 and 1998 and will host group matches and one Round of 16 game at EURO 2016.

FRANCE
GROUP A

France have regularly made their mark on the UEFA European Football Championship, appearing at the first tournament in 1960 and twice becoming champions. The captain of their victorious EURO 2000 side, Didier Deschamps, now leads the team as head coach. The squad is packed with talent, from experienced goalkeeper Hugo Lloris and exciting defenders such as Raphaël Varane, to skilful midfielders Yohan Cabaye and Morgan Schneiderlin. Up front, the French possess plenty of pace and power with Loic Rémy, Olivier Giroud, Anthony Martial and Antoine Griezmann all vying for starting places.

FACT FILE

COACH:
Didier Deschamps
FIRST INTERNATIONAL:
1904, v Belgium
NATIONAL STADIUM:
Stade de France
NICKNAME: Les Bleus,
Les Tricolores
EUROS APPEARANCES:
Nine
ROUTE TO EURO 2016:
Hosts
BEST FINISH: Champions
(1984, 2000)
ONES TO WATCH: Paul
Pogba, Olivier Giroud,
Hugo Lloris, Blaise Matuidi,
Raphaël Varane

SUPER STAT
France hold the record for most goals scored at a EURO – 14 in 1984. Nine of them were scored by Michel Platini.

Midfielder Yohan Cabaye drives away from an Albanian opponent during a 1-1 friendly draw.

Goalkeeper Hugo Lloris has been France's captain since EURO 2012.

Defender Raphaël Varane (4) scored the winner against Sweden in late 2014.

ROMANIA
GROUP A

Romania's EURO high point came in 2000, when they knocked out Germany and England before losing to Italy in the quarter-finals. Coached by Romanian legend Anghel Iordănescu since 2014 (his third spell in charge), the Tricolours were defensively strong in their Group F campaign. With defenders such as inspirational captain Răvzan Raț, Paul Papp and Vlad Chiricheș to the fore, Romania did not lose a single qualifier, and prevented group winners Northern Ireland from scoring in their two games. To do well at EURO 2016, however, the Romanians will need to match their defensive resilience with more forward firepower.

FACT FILE

COACH:
Anghel Iordănescu
FIRST INTERNATIONAL:
1922, v Yugoslavia
NATIONAL STADIUM:
Arena Natională
NICKNAME: Tricolorii
(The Tricolours)
EUROS APPEARANCES:
Five
ROUTE TO EURO 2016:
Group F runners-up
BEST FINISH: Quarter-finals (2000)
ONES TO WATCH:
Bogdan Stancu, Vlad Chiricheș, Alexandru Maxim, Gabriel Torje

Defender Paul Papp scored both goals when Romania inflicted Northern Ireland's sole defeat in qualifying.

Romania enter EURO 2016 not having lost a competitive game since 2013.

SUPER STAT
Romania conceded only two goals in their ten qualifying games for EURO 2016 – the fewest of any side.

Ovidiu Hoban scores a last-gasp equaliser in added time versus Finland.

ALBANIA
GROUP A

Albania's long wait to reach a major international tournament finally ended in Yerevan, Armenia in October 2015. Their 3-0 away victory secured EURO 2016 qualification and pushed 1992 champions Denmark into the play-offs. Managed by former Torino and Udinese coach Gianni De Biasi since 2011, Albania have become a defensive powerhouse marshalled by their captain, Lorik Cana. The Eagles' qualifying campaign began with a sensational 1-0 away win over Portugal and their excellent away record continued. Resilient defending and a friendly victory over France gave Albania their highest-ever FIFA world ranking in August 2015 – 22nd in the world.

FACT FILE

COACH: Gianni De Biasi
FIRST INTERNATIONAL: 1946, v Yugoslavia
NATIONAL STADIUM: Elbasan Arena
NICKNAME: Shqiponjat (The Eagles)
EUROS APPEARANCES: One
ROUTE TO EURO 2016: Group I runners-up
BEST FINISH: n/a
ONES TO WATCH: Lorik Cana, Hamdi Salihi, Odise Roshi

SUPER STAT
Albania averaged 45 per cent possession during qualification for EURO 2016 – the lowest of any qualifying team.

Bekim Balaj (19) scores the winner against Portugal in Albania's first qualifying game.

Albania line up before a 1-0 friendly victory over France in 2015.

Vastly experienced captain Lorik Cana's international debut came in 2003, in a qualifier for EURO 2004.

SWITZERLAND
GROUP A

EURO '96 saw the first appearance of Switzerland at the finals tournament, where they started well with a 1-1 draw with hosts England. They have won just one out of eight group games since then, but Swiss fans have high expectations of the latest side thanks to experienced campaigners such as Johan Djourou in defence and athletic, creative midfielders Gökhan Inler and Xherdan Shaqiri (scorer of five goals during qualifying). Switzerland scored 24 goals in qualifying under the former Lazio coach Vladimir Petković, and will need to keep up their goalscoring if they are to progress out of their group.

FACT FILE

COACH:
Vladimir Petković
FIRST INTERNATIONAL:
1905, v France
NATIONAL STADIUM: n/a
NICKNAME: Nati Suisse,
The Schweizer Nati
EUROS APPEARANCES:
Four
ROUTE TO EURO 2016:
Group E runners-up
BEST FINISH: 4th in
group (1996, 2004, 2008)
ONES TO WATCH:
Xherdan Shaqiri, Breel
Embolo, Johan Djourou,
Stephan Lichtsteiner

SUPER STAT
Switzerland's biggest victories in European internationals have both come against San Marino – 7-0 in 1991 and 2015.

Switzerland celebrate a 7-0 win over San Marino which featured seven different goalscorers.

Gökhan Inler's versatility allows him to break down opposition moves and launch attacks for his own side.

The Swiss pose before the crucial 3-2 win over Slovenia which helped them secure second place in Group E.

ENGLAND
GROUP B

While England's clubs and leagues are very strong, the national team has often struggled at tournaments. The brightest England EURO performances were at EURO '96 where they narrowly lost a semi-final penalty shoot-out against Germany. In recent seasons, the retirement of senior players such as Steven Gerrard and Frank Lampard has seen the development of a young side managed by experienced coach Roy Hodgson. It possesses attacking talents such as Raheem Sterling, Daniel Sturridge and Wayne Rooney, with Joe Hart providing solidity in goal. Under Hodgson, England cruised through their EURO 2016 qualifying group, winning all ten games, and are likely to prove stiff opponents at the finals tournament.

All eyes will be on Raheem Sterling after his £49m move to Manchester City, a record fee for an English player.

Harry Kane scored just 79 seconds into his debut, in a 4-0 win over Lithuania in March 2015.

SUPER STAT
Nine footballers have played over 100 times for England. They include Wayne Rooney (109 caps), David Beckham (115) and Peter Shilton (125).

England's first EURO 2016 qualifier was a 2-0 away win over Switzerland.

RUSSIA
GROUP B

Russia was a major part of the Soviet Union team that took part in five UEFA European Football Championships, reaching the final four times and winning the trophy once. They made their EUROs debut as Russia in 1996. At EURO 2008, inspired by Andrey Arshavin, they beat Sweden, Greece and the Netherlands to reach the semi-finals. During EURO 2016 qualifying, Artem Dzyuba scored eight times, including four in a 7-0 thrashing of Liechtenstein. He, along with Aleksandr Kokorin and, possibly, veteran Aleksandr Kerzhakov (Russia's leading goalscorer), will need to find the scoresheet if the team are to do well in France.

SUPER STAT
Russia and the Soviet Union have scored 250 goals in UEFA European Football Championship qualifying and finals matches.

Two first-half goals against Montenegro secured Russia's qualification for EURO 2016.

Artem Dzyuba scores the winner in the crucial home qualifier against Sweden, who finished two points behind Russia.

EURO 2016 will be young striker Alexsandr Kokorin's second finals tournament, after he played two games at EURO 2012.

WALES
GROUP B

Wales will make their debut at the EUROs on the back of a series of outstanding performances during qualifying. These included an epic 1-0 victory over Belgium in June 2015, a side ranked at the time by FIFA as the second best in the world. Gareth Bale scored the winning goal in that match – his 50th appearance for Wales – and he is the player other teams fear the most. Yet the entire side, coached by Chris Coleman and captained by Ashley Williams, offers threats throughout, from Arsenal midfielder Aaron Ramsey's powerful runs and shooting, to Joe Ledley's hard running and Joe Allen's slick passing.

Vice-captain Aaron Ramsey made his Wales debut at the age of just 17.

SUPER STAT
Wales' most famous EURO qualifying victory came in 1991 over world champions Germany via a goal from Ian Rush, Wales' all-time top-scorer (28 goals).

In 2010 Wales were ranked 112 by FIFA. In autumn 2015 they reached the top 10.

Gareth Bale celebrates scoring the winner against Belgium in June 2015.

SLOVAKIA
GROUP B

Until 1993, many Slovakian footballers played for the Czechoslovakian national team. In fact, eight of the players in the Czech team that beat West Germany to win the 1976 UEFA European Football Championship came from Slovakia. As an independent nation, Slovakia have struggled to qualify for tournaments, but hurtled through the early stages of qualifying for EURO 2016 with six straight wins in a row. These included away wins in Ukraine and Belarus and a victory over defending champions Spain, thanks to a strong defence organized by Liverpool defender Martin Škrtel and crafty attacking play led by Marek Hamšík.

FACT FILE

COACH:
Ján Kozák
FIRST INTERNATIONAL:
1939, v Germany
NATIONAL STADIUM:
Štadión pod Dubňom
NICKNAME: Repre
EUROS APPEARANCES:
One
ROUTE TO EURO 2016:
Group C runners-up
BEST FINISH: n/a
ONES TO WATCH: Marek Hamšík, Róbert Vittek, Martin Škrtel

Martin Škrtel clears the ball during Slovakia's momentous win over Spain.

Slovakia will be looking to surprise more experienced teams at EURO 2016.

Juraj Kucka (centre) scored Slovakia's first goal in their 2-1 win over Spain.

SUPER STAT
Slovakian midfielder Vladimir Weiss's father and grandfather both played for Czechoslovakia and were both called Vladimir Weiss!

21

GERMANY
GROUP C

Since winning on their tournament debut in 1972, Germany have been the EUROs' most consistent performers. As Germany or West Germany, they have been champions three times, were runners-up in 1976, 1992 and 2008, and have reached the semi-finals eight times in total. Joachim Löw's side enter EURO 2016 as world champions, and despite shock losses to Poland and the Republic of Ireland during qualifying, they remain one of the favourites to reach the final. With firepower and guile from midfielders such as Thomas Müller, Toni Kroos and Mesut Özil, and the world's best goalkeeper in Manuel Neuer, expectations of a fourth title are understandably high.

FACT FILE

COACH:
Joachim Löw
FIRST INTERNATIONAL:
1908, v Switzerland
NATIONAL STADIUM: n/a
NICKNAME: Die
Mannschaft (The Team)
EUROS APPEARANCES:
Twelve
ROUTE TO EURO 2016:
Group D winners
BEST FINISH: Champions
(1972, 1980, 1996)
ONES TO WATCH:
Thomas Müller, Toni Kroos,
Mario Götze, Manuel Neuer

Captain Bastian Schweinsteiger controls the ball during Germany's 3-2 away victory over Scotland.

Mario Götze celebrates after scoring the first of two goals in Germany's 3-1 defeat of Poland.

André Schürrle (9) scored a hat-trick in Germany's 7-0 win over Gibraltar.

SUPER STAT
No team has played more games (43), won more games (23) or scored more goals (65) at the EURO finals than Germany.

UKRAINE
GROUP C

As a former Soviet republic, Ukraine provided many superb players to the Soviet Union national team, most notably at the 1988 EURO tournament. The 20-man squad that reached the final that year contained 12 Ukrainians. As an independent nation, Ukraine first appeared at the tournament in 2012 as co-hosts with Poland. In EURO 2016 qualifying, a loss to Slovakia and two defeats to Spain left Ukraine in the play-offs, where they qualified with a 2-0 win at home and 1-1 away draw against Slovenia. Mykhaylo Fomenko's side possess bundles of experience and goal potential from players such as Andriy Yarmolenko and Yevhen Seleznyov, but will need to be at their very best to get out of their group.

FACT FILE

COACH:
Mykhaylo Fomenko
FIRST INTERNATIONAL:
1992, v Hungary
NATIONAL STADIUM:
NSC Olimpiyskiy
NICKNAME: The Yellow and Blues
EUROS APPEARANCES: Two
ROUTE TO EURO 2016:
Play-offs v Slovenia
BEST FINISH: 3rd in group (2012)
ONES TO WATCH:
Anatoliy Tymoshchuk, Yevhen Seleznyov, Yevhen Konoplyanka, Andriy Yarmolenko

Anatoliy Tymoshchuk is a veteran of Ukraine's 2006 FIFA World Cup and EURO 2012 campaigns.

Ukraine conceded just four goals in their entire ten-game EURO 2016 qualifying campaign.

The team celebrate qualifying after Andriy Yarmolenko's goal in the 7th minute of injury time against Slovenia.

SUPER STAT
Ukraine's captain, Anatoliy Tymoshchuk, is their most-capped player, with 141 appearances for his country.

POLAND
GROUP C

It took 13 attempts to qualify for the EUROs before Poland finally made their debut in 2008. The Poles then co-hosted EURO 2012 with Ukraine. Fans are hoping it will be third-time lucky for a team blessed with Robert Lewandowski – a goalscorer in his absolute prime. The Bayern Munich hitman notched up an incredible 13 goals and four assists as Poland scored 33 times in qualifying – more than any other side. To succeed in France, Lewandowski and other attacking players such as Jakub Błaszczykowski and Arkadiusz Milik will need good service. At the back, Poland boast a trio of talented goalkeepers: Artur Boruc, Łukasz Fabiański and Wojciech Szczęsny.

Poland line up before a 1-1 draw with the Republic of Ireland in Dublin.

SUPER STAT
In October 2014 Poland became the first team in 33 EURO qualifying games to defeat Germany, with a 2-0 win.

Arkadiusz Milik scores in Poland's famous 2-0 win, their first ever victory over Germany.

Łukasz Fabiański celebrates as Poland secure a crucial point in a 2-2 draw away to Scotland.

NORTHERN IRELAND
GROUP C

After decades of heartbreak, in 2015 Northern Ireland qualified for their first EURO finals tournament by beating Greece 3-1 in Group F. The Green and Whites got off to a flying start, winning their first three games, and completed the ten qualifiers with only one defeat. Reliant on a strong defence – containing experienced players such as Gareth McAuley, Aaron Hughes and Jonny Evans – Northern Ireland will need to ally the skill and energy of midfielders Chris Brunt and skipper Steven Davis to the goalscoring threat of Kyle Lafferty in order to do well in France.

FACT FILE

COACH:
Michael O'Neill
FIRST INTERNATIONAL:
1953, v Scotland
NATIONAL STADIUM:
Windsor Park
NICKNAME: Norn Iron, Green and White Army
EUROS APPEARANCES: One
ROUTE TO EURO 2016: Group F winners
BEST FINISH: n/a
ONES TO WATCH: Steven Davis, Kyle Lafferty, Jonny Evans, Josh Magennis

Captain Steven Davis scored twice in the 3-1 win over Greece that guaranteed qualification.

Northern Ireland, with Roy Carroll in goal, line up before their away game versus Romania.

SUPER STAT
Defender Aaron Hughes has appeared in 32 EURO qualifiers – more than any other Northern Irish player. He has 96 caps in total for his country.

Striker Josh Magennis celebrates qualification. Until 2008, he was a goalkeeper.

SPAIN
GROUP D

Spain's long wait for a repeat of their 1964 EURO glory finally came in 2008. It signalled the start of a golden period, which saw them become FIFA World Cup winners in 2010 and, in 2012, the first team to win the EUROs back-to-back. While they endured a tough 2014 FIFA World Cup, expectation for EURO 2016 remains high. A clutch of skilful and creative midfielders, such as Andrés Iniesta, David Silva, Santi Cazorla and Juan Mata, are expected to both create and score goals. At the back, the experienced Sergio Ramos, Gerard Piqué and long-serving goalkeeper Iker Casillas will need to be at their very best for Spain to prosper.

David Silva scores the first of Spain's four goals in the EURO 2012 final versus Italy.

Andrés Iniesta was the player of the tournament at EURO 2012.

SUPER STAT
The 23-man UEFA Team of the Tournament in 2012 featured ten Spanish players including Fernando Torres, one of the six joint top-scorers with three goals.

Iker Casillas (1) poses with the Spain side he captained to victory over Belarus.

CZECH REPUBLIC
GROUP D

A 2-1 away win over Latvia in September 2015 confirmed the Czech Republic's record of qualifying for every EURO since the country's formation in 1993. Their debut in 1996 saw victories over Italy, Portugal and France to reach the final. They almost repeated the feat in 2004 when, propelled by five goals from tournament top-scorer Milan Baroš, they beat Germany and the Netherlands, but lost to Greece at the semi-final stage. Under former FC Viktoria Plzeň coach Pavel Vrba, and with a blend of experience and youth, the Czechs will hope to at least match their 2012 performance and reach the quarter-finals.

FACT FILE

COACH: Pavel Vrba
FIRST INTERNATIONAL: 1994, v Turkey
NATIONAL STADIUM: n/a
NICKNAME: Národ'ák (the National Team), Cesti Lvi (the Czech Lions)
EUROS APPEARANCES: Six
ROUTE TO EURO 2016: Group A winners
BEST FINISH: Runners-up (1996)
ONES TO WATCH: Petr Čech, Bořek Dočkal, David Lafata

Bořek Dočkal (9) celebrates with Pavel Kadeřábek after scoring the winner against Turkey in October 2014.

The Czech team captained by Petr Čech (in yellow).

SUPER STAT
At EURO 2012, the Czech Republic became the first team to win a EURO group with a negative goal difference (−1).

Veteran midfielder Tomáš Rosický has over 100 caps for the Czechs.

TURKEY
GROUP D

Turkey qualified as the best third-placed team in the qualifying groups. Selçuk İnan's curled free-kick, just a minute from full time, earned the Crescent-Stars a last-gasp win over Group A leaders Iceland to book their place in France. They started the campaign with back-to-back defeats, but epic victories over the Netherlands and the Czech Republic cemented their reputation as comeback kings, having previously come back against the Czech Republic and Croatia at EURO 2008 before losing to Germany in the semi-finals. Turkish fans fervently hope that stars such as Arda Turan and Hakan Çalhanoğlu will inspire Turkey to another series of rousing performances.

FACT FILE

COACH:
Fatih Terim
FIRST INTERNATIONAL:
1923, v Romania
NATIONAL STADIUM: n/a
NICKNAME:
Ay-Yıldızlılar
(The Crescent-Stars)
EUROS APPEARANCES:
Four
ROUTE TO EURO 2016:
Best third-place finisher
BEST FINISH: Semi-finals
(2008)
ONES TO WATCH: Arda Turan, Selçuk İnan, Burak Yılmaz, Hakan Çalhanoğlu

SUPER STAT
Fatih Terim is in charge for his third spell. He has managed Turkey for 119 matches, in addition to 25 games as Turkey's U-21 head coach.

Turkish players salute their fans after a dramatic win over Iceland secured qualification.

Hakan Çalhanoğlu scored his first goal for Turkey in the Group A game against the Czech Republic.

Turkey were unbeaten in their last eight qualifying games to reach France.

NO TO RACISM
RESPECT

CROATIA
GROUP D

Croatia supplied the Yugoslavian national team with many outstanding footballers before independence in 1991. They have since proved a major force in European football, with their distinctive red-and-white chequered shirts present at four previous EUROs. At EURO '96 Croatia suffered a narrow quarter-final defeat to Germany, but revenge came quickly as they knocked Germany out of the 1998 FIFA World Cup with a 3-0 win. Although the current side only guaranteed qualification in their last match, hopes are high that their blend of rugged defence and midfield scheming from players such as Ivan Rakitić and Luka Modrić will see them through to the knockout stages.

Barcelona midfielder Ivan Rakitić debuted for Croatia in 2007 and has scored ten goals in 75 appearances.

Croatia managed a pair of 1-1 draws against group winners Italy during qualification.

Croatian hopes rest partly on striker Mario Mandžukić, here scoring his 19th international goal past Italy's Gianluigi Buffon.

SUPER STAT
Croatia have lost only seven of the 52 EURO qualifying matches they have played since their formation, scoring 98 goals.

BELGIUM
GROUP E

Considering the number of talented players produced by Belgium, it's a surprise that EURO 2016 is their first finals appearance since 2000. After failing to reach EURO 2012, they went on a 14-game winning streak in 2012-13 and entered the 2015-16 season ranked second in the world by FIFA. Marshalled by experienced defenders including captain Vincent Kompany, Belgium boast a wealth of attackers, many of whom – Eden Hazard, Kevin De Bruyne, Nacer Chadli and Christian Benteke – play in the English Premier League. With this exciting mix of players available to Marc Wilmots, fans of the Red Devils will hope for a strong showing.

FACT FILE

COACH:
Marc Wilmots
FIRST INTERNATIONAL:
1904, v France
NATIONAL STADIUM:
King Baudouin Stadium
NICKNAME: Les Diables Rouges (The Red Devils)
EUROS APPEARANCES:
Five
ROUTE TO EURO 2016:
Group B winners
BEST FINISH: Runners-up (1980)
ONES TO WATCH: Eden Hazard, Christian Benteke, Kevin De Bruyne, Romelu Lukaku

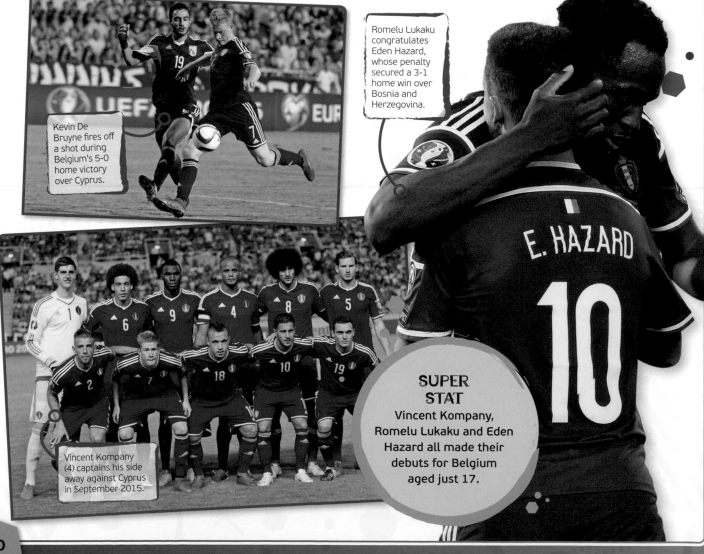

Kevin De Bruyne fires off a shot during Belgium's 5-0 home victory over Cyprus.

Romelu Lukaku congratulates Eden Hazard, whose penalty secured a 3-1 home win over Bosnia and Herzegovina.

Vincent Kompany (4) captains his side away against Cyprus in September 2015.

SUPER STAT
Vincent Kompany, Romelu Lukaku and Eden Hazard all made their debuts for Belgium aged just 17.

ITALY
GROUP E

Europe's most successful FIFA World Cup team (equal with Germany) have triumphed just once at the UEFA European Football Championships, back in 1968. They have come close on other occasions, making the final in 2000 and then in 2012 after beating Germany in the semi-final. The Azzurri won seven and drew three of their ten qualifying matches for EURO 2016 – a testament to their hardworking defence led by the gritty Giorgio Chiellini and Gianluigi Buffon in goal. To reach the knockout stages, coach Antonio Conte will need to blend exciting young talent such as Stephan El Shaarawy, Domenico Berardi and Marco Verratti with more experienced players, including the veteran playmaker Andrea Pirlo.

FACT FILE

COACH: Antonio Conte
FIRST INTERNATIONAL: 1910, v France
NATIONAL STADIUM: n/a
NICKNAME: Azzurri (Blues)
EUROS APPEARANCES: Nine
ROUTE TO EURO 2016: Group H winners
BEST FINISH: Champions (1968)
ONES TO WATCH: Gianluigi Buffon, Giorgio Chiellini, Stephan El Shaarawy, Andrea Pirlo, Graziano Pellè

Stephan El Shaarawy's first goal in qualifying was scored in a 3-1 away win over Azerbaijan.

Italy went unbeaten in qualifying, with seven wins and three draws in their ten games.

Midfielder Claudio Marchisio started every game at EURO 2012 as Italy reached the final.

SUPER STAT
Italy have won 77 and lost just 19 of their EURO qualifying and finals tournament matches, scoring 204 goals in total.

REPUBLIC OF IRELAND
GROUP E

The Republic secured a play-off win over Bosnia and Herzegovina with two goals from Jon Walters in front of a delirious home crowd. It capped a rollercoaster ride through a very tough group with just two defeats, an unbeaten home record and a superb win and a draw against Germany. Coach Martin O'Neill must rely on experienced players such as John O'Shea in defence and Jon Walters and Robbie Keane in attack. But there is also a clutch of promising young players, especially in midfield, where James McCarthy and Robbie Brady may make names for themselves at EURO 2016.

The Republic line up before their play-off match versus Bosnia and Herzegovina.

SUPER STAT
Striker Robbie Keane is the Republic's most-capped player (143) and top scorer (67 goals – 53 ahead of Kevin Doyle and Shane Long).

Robbie Brady scored during the play-offs and will be hoping to strike again at EURO 2016.

Shane Long scores in the 70th minute to record a memorable October 2015 victory against Germany in qualifying.

SWEDEN
GROUP E

Sweden's best EURO performance was at their debut tournament in 1992, when they beat England and eventual champions Denmark before losing 3-2 to Germany in the semi-finals. The Swedes reached the quarter-finals in 2004, recording their highest finals scoreline (5-0 against Bulgaria) before going out 5-4 in a penalty shoot-out to the Netherlands. The current side relies heavily on the unpredictable genius of striker Zlatan Ibrahimović, whose 11 goals during qualifying proved crucial. But they have other attacking talents, with experienced playmaking midfielders such as Kim Källström, Erkan Zengin and Sebastian Larsson, backed up by ten-time Swedish goalkeeper of the year, Andreas Isaksson.

FACT FILE

COACH: Erik Hamrén
FIRST INTERNATIONAL: 1908, v Norway
NATIONAL STADIUM: Friends Arena
NICKNAME: Blågult (Blue-Yellows)
EUROS APPEARANCES: Six
ROUTE TO EURO 2016: Play-offs v Denmark
BEST FINISH: Semi-finals (1992)
ONES TO WATCH: Zlatan Ibrahimović, Kim Källström, Sebastian Larsson

Sebastian Larsson appeared in 11 EURO 2016 qualifying games as well as the 2008 and 2012 tournaments.

Team-mates rush to celebrate with Zlatan Ibrahimović after Sweden qualify for EURO 2016.

Sweden failed to score in just one of their 12 EURO 2016 qualifying or play-off games.

SUPER STAT
Sweden have played 121 UEFA European Football Championship games in tournaments and qualifying, scoring 198 goals.

PORTUGAL
GROUP F

Portugal's appearances at UEFA European Football Championships have tended to be eventful. Inspired by the great Luís Figo, they reached the final at EURO 2004, and at EURO 2012 beat Denmark, the Netherlands and the Czech Republic on the way to the semi-finals. Portugal have always progressed out of their group and hopes will be high again in France. Europe's greatest footballer, Cristiano Ronaldo, and other attacking midfielders including João Moutinho and the captain Nani offer significant threats in front of goal. At the back, veterans Pepe, Bruno Alves and Fábio Coentrão are likely to keep things tight. The Portuguese can expect to fare well provided Ronaldo isn't shackled.

Now Portugal's captain, Nani scored on his debut against Denmark in 2006.

All of Portugal's seven wins out of eight EURO 2016 qualifiers were by a single-goal margin.

Cristiano Ronaldo struck five times in EURO 2016 qualifying.

SUPER STAT
Portugal have reached at least the semi-finals in four out of the six EUROs they have played in.

ICELAND
GROUP F

In June 2012, Iceland were ranked 131st in the world by FIFA. Since then, under coaches Lars Lagerbäck and Heimir Hallgrímsson, they narrowly missed qualifying for the 2014 FIFA World Cup and in October 2015 reached their highest ever FIFA world ranking – 23rd, above Denmark and Sweden. With attacking talents in midfield such as Gylfi Sigurðsson and forwards like Kolbeinn Sigþórsson, Iceland set qualifying Group A alight. Sensationally, they beat the Netherlands both home and away on their way to a runners-up spot, making it to the UEFA European Football Championship finals for the very first time.

Gylfi Sigurðsson starred against the Netherlands, scoring all three goals in the two games.

Kolbeinn Sigþórsson rounds a Czech defender to score in a 2-1 win in June 2015.

SUPER STAT
Eiður Guðjohnsen made his Iceland debut in a 1996 friendly versus Estonia, coming on as a substitute for his father, Arnór Guðjohnsen!

Eiður Guðjohnsen is Iceland's top-scorer, with 25 goals in 81 games.

AUSTRIA
GROUP F

Austria took part in qualifying for the very first EURO tournament but were knocked out by France, 9-4 on aggregate. It would be 48 years before they managed to qualify – as hosts for EURO 2008. Coached since 2011 by former Swiss midfielder Marcel Koller, Austria combine a strong defence organized by their captain, Christian Fuchs, with pace out wide and clever players in the centre such as Marko Arnautović and Martin Harnik. A pair of 1-0 victories over Russia during qualifying marked the Austrians out as a side that is highly competitive and hard to break down.

FACT FILE

COACH: Marcel Koller
FIRST INTERNATIONAL: 1902, v Hungary
NATIONAL STADIUM: Ernst-Happel-Stadion
NICKNAME: Das Team
EUROS APPEARANCES: Two
ROUTE TO EURO 2016: Group G winners
BEST FINISH: Third in group (2008)
ONES TO WATCH: David Alaba, Marc Janko, Martin Harnik, Marko Arnautović

Austria line up before a 1-0 home win over Russia with a goal from substitute Rubin Okotie.

Striker Marko Arnautović has over 45 caps for Austria.

Marc Janko scores a spectacular overhead goal against Russia in June 2015.

HUNGARY
GROUP F

The 2016 finals tournament will feature Hungary for the first time since 1972. The Hungarians had one of the greatest teams of the 1950s and early 1960s, winning three Olympic gold medals and finishing runners-up in the 1954 FIFA World Cup. Later teams were not so successful, but the current crop of players has proved to be strong defensively, with four wins and four draws from ten games securing third place in Group F. German coach Bernd Storck will need to coax strong performances from his squad, which contains veteran players such as midfielder Zoltán Gera, defender Roland Juhász and captain Balázs Dzsudzsák.

Veteran keeper Gábor Király instructs his defence during the play-off match against Norway.

SUPER STAT
If goalkeeper Gábor Király plays at EURO 2016, he will become the competition's oldest-ever player at over 40 years of age.

EURO 2016 will be Hungary's first major tournament since the 1986 FIFA World Cup.

Bernd Storck is thrown into the air as Hungary celebrate a 3-1 play-off triumph.

GOALKEEPERS

THIBAUT COURTOIS

COUNTRY: Belgium
DATE OF BIRTH: 11.05.92
CLUB: Chelsea
CAPS: 32
GOALS: 0

PLAYER PROFILE
Courtois is considered one of the best young goalkeepers in world football. He played on loan for Atlético Madrid for three seasons before returning to his parent club Chelsea in 2014, where he ousted the highly rated Petr Čech from the starting lineup.

SKILLS
Courtois has modelled his calm, unflappable goalkeeping style on his childhood hero, Edwin van der Sar of the Netherlands. Tall yet extremely agile, Courtois is still learning the game, but he is excellent under the high ball and is a strong shot-stopper.

GIANLUIGI BUFFON

COUNTRY: Italy
DATE OF BIRTH: 28.01.78
CLUB: Juventus
CAPS: 154
GOALS: 0

PLAYER PROFILE
Buffon became the world's most expensive keeper after his £32.6-million transfer from Parma in 2001, and has kept more than 250 Serie A clean sheets. A veteran of three previous EUROs, he was voted into UEFA's Team of the Tournament in 2008 and 2012.

SKILLS
Buffon's long-running success is down to his consistency, excellent concentration and his superb agility that allows him to make quick reaction saves. He is a masterful organiser of his defence and uses his experience and positioning to close down threats on his goal.

PETR ČECH

COUNTRY: Czech Republic
DATE OF BIRTH: 20.05.82
CLUB: Arsenal
CAPS: 118
GOALS: 0

PLAYER PROFILE
Čech is a highly experienced keeper who has been voted Czech Footballer of the Year a record seven times. He joined Arsenal in 2015 after 11 seasons and 220 clean sheets with Chelsea. He was selected for UEFA's Team of the Tournament at EURO 2004.

SKILLS
Currently the Czech Republic's most-capped player, Čech is a solid, calm keeper with excellent concentration and outstanding shot-stopping skills. He communicates well with his defence and has a great command of his penalty area.

MANUEL NEUER

COUNTRY: Germany
DATE OF BIRTH: 27.03.86
CLUB: Bayern Munich
CAPS: 63
GOALS: 0

PLAYER PROFILE
Europe's best goalkeeper has won almost everything in the game, from the UEFA Champions League with Bayern Munich to the 2014 FIFA World Cup, where he was voted the tournament's top keeper. Only a EURO winners' medal has eluded him so far.

SKILLS
Confident and commanding, Neuer is brave, has lightning reactions and is an expert penalty-saver. He often plays outside his area as a 'sweeper-keeper', snuffing out opposition attempts on goal and using his excellent ball skills to turn defence into attack.

DEFENDERS

GIORGIO CHIELLINI

COUNTRY: Italy
DATE OF BIRTH: 14.08.84
CLUB: Juventus
CAPS: 82
GOALS: 6

PLAYER PROFILE
A EURO 2012 runner-up with Italy, Chiellini is considered one of the toughest and best defenders in Europe. He has notched up almost 400 games for Juventus, with whom he has won four Serie A titles and a UEFA Champions League runners-up medal.

SKILLS
Tough and rugged, Chiellini is a dominant central defender, good at marking powerful opposing strikers and challenging hard for the ball. He is especially strong in the air, making towering headers both in defence and in attack.

LORIK CANA

COUNTRY: Albania
DATE OF BIRTH: 27.07.83
CLUB: Nantes
CAPS: 89
GOALS: 1

PLAYER PROFILE
A three-time Albanian footballer of the year, Cana has enjoyed spells at Paris Saint-Germain, Olympique de Marseille, Sunderland, Galatasaray and Lazio. Appointed captain of Albania in 2011, he is his country's record caps holder.

SKILLS
Cana is a hugely versatile footballer, able to play as a defender but also as a defensive midfielder. His never-say-die attitude and high level of stamina see him break up many opposition attacks, often with his sharp, incisive tackling.

DAVID ALABA

COUNTRY: Austria
DATE OF BIRTH: 24.06.92
CLUB: Bayern Munich
CAPS: 42
GOALS: 11

PLAYER PROFILE

Alaba is one of a new breed of extremely versatile players able to play on the left or right in defence or midfield. A key player for Bayern Munich, he has been picked as the best left-back in Europe for two UEFA Teams of the Year in succession.

SKILLS

Alaba can power forwards in attack or track back in defence where he is a clean, committed tackler. He has excellent ball skills and an eye for goal – he finished Austria's 2014 FIFA World Cup qualification campaign as the team's highest scorer, with six goals.

MATS HUMMELS

COUNTRY: Germany
DATE OF BIRTH: 16.12.88
CLUB: Borussia Dortmund
CAPS: 44
GOALS: 4

PLAYER PROFILE

Hummels joined Dortmund from Bayern Munich in 2009 and went on to win the Bundesliga twice. He debuted for Germany in 2010 and played every minute of Germany's EURO 2012 campaign. Hummels was selected for the FIFA 2014 World Cup Team of the Tournament.

SKILLS

As the leader of the defence, he is a good header of the ball and is skilled at timing his challenges to break up opposition attacks. He's also comfortable on the ball and able to move forwards to link defence and attack.

DEFENDERS

VINCENT KOMPANY

COUNTRY: Belgium
DATE OF BIRTH: 10.04.86
CLUB: Manchester City
CAPS: 72
GOALS: 4

PLAYER PROFILE
Captain of his club and country, Kompany has won two league titles in both Belgium and England and is widely considered one of the best central defenders in Europe. He is also owner and chairman of Belgian fourth division football club BX Brussels.

SKILLS
A powerful, athletic defender, Kompany is renowned for his clear, calm leadership and his ability to anticipate an opposing attacker's movements. He is a strong, clean tackler and is commanding in the air, where he wins most aerial battles with opposing strikers.

ASHLEY WILLIAMS

COUNTRY: Wales
DATE OF BIRTH: 23.08.84
CLUB: Swansea City
CAPS: 56
GOALS: 1

PLAYER PROFILE
Williams has been a part of Swansea's rise to become an established English Premier League side since joining from Stockport County in 2008. The highly rated central defender is captain of his club and has led his country since 2012.

SKILLS
Strong, determined and dependable, Williams has missed less than a dozen games in seven seasons with Swansea. He is a natural leader, calm and dependable under pressure, a strong tackler and capable of marking top strikers out of the game.

SERGIO RAMOS

COUNTRY: Spain
DATE OF BIRTH: 30.03.86
CLUB: Real Madrid
CAPS: 130
GOALS: 10

PLAYER PROFILE

Ramos became the youngest European player to reach 100 caps for his country at the age of 26. He played as a full-back or central defender in Spain's winning sides at EURO 2008 and EURO 2012, as well as winning the FIFA World Cup in 2010.

SKILLS

Ramos is a strong, physical defender and a tough tackler with the pace to chase down opponents, while his aerial ability makes him a threat during set pieces. He has scored in Spain's last three UEFA European Football Championship qualifying campaigns.

RĂZVAN RAŢ

COUNTRY: Romania
DATE OF BIRTH: 26.05.81
CLUB: Rayo Vallecano
CAPS: 108
GOALS: 2

PLAYER PROFILE

A seven-times winner of the Ukrainian Premier League with Shakhtar Donetsk, Raţ has been the Romanian captain since 2011. Playing as a left-back, he earned his 100th cap for his country in 2014 in a 2-0 win over Finland during qualifying for EURO 2016.

SKILLS

Raţ uses his vast experience to read the game well. He is disciplined, strong and able to track opposing attackers as they make threatening runs. He rarely scores goals, but helps launch attacks with long passes to his team-mates upfield.

MIDFIELDERS

JAKUB BŁASZCZYKOWSKI

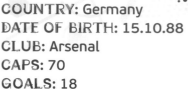

COUNTRY: Poland
DATE OF BIRTH: 14.12.85
CLUB: Fiorentina
CAPS: 75
GOALS: 15

PLAYER PROFILE
Captain of Poland at EURO 2012, Jakub Błaszczykowski made his international debut in 2006. A year later, he moved to Borussia Dortmund, where he was player of the year and won the Bundesliga, before going on loan in 2015 to Italian side Fiorentina.

SKILLS
He is renowned as a hard-working, strong and tenacious player who battles hard to win the ball and then uses it aggressively. Playing as a wide midfielder, usually on the right, he aims to deliver pinpoint crosses and passes to team-mates.

MESUT ÖZIL

COUNTRY: Germany
DATE OF BIRTH: 15.10.88
CLUB: Arsenal
CAPS: 70
GOALS: 18

PLAYER PROFILE
The former FC Schalke 04, Werder Bremen and Real Madrid midfielder is a three-time winner of the German player of the year award, and won the FIFA World Cup in 2014. He also scored in the final of the 2009 UEFA European Under-21 Championship.

SKILLS
Well-known for his skill and finesse on the ball, Özil is adept at keeping possession and launching attacks. He can pass accurately with either foot, though he often favours his left to make dazzling assists and other telling passes for his team-mates.

ARÐA TURAN

COUNTRY: Turkey
DATE OF BIRTH: 30.01.87
CLUB: Barcelona
CAPS: 87
GOALS: 16

PLAYER PROFILE

A three-time Turkish footballer of the year (2008, 2009, 2014), this creative attacking midfielder played for Galatasaray and Atlético Madrid before joining Barcelona in 2015 for a fee of €32 million.

SKILLS

Great on the ball, Turan can dribble through the tightest gaps or pass accurately to set up goals for team-mates. He scored or made an assist in four of Turkey's last five qualifying matches for EURO 2016, a run that included a superb individual goal in the crucial 3-0 win over the Netherlands.

GYLFI SIGURÐSSON

COUNTRY: Iceland
DATE OF BIRTH: 08.09.89
CLUB: Swansea City
CAPS: 35
GOALS: 12

PLAYER PROFILE

After leaving Reading for Germany, Sigurðsson then returned to England to play for Tottenham Hotspur and Swansea City. He is a favourite with fans, especially after scoring three goals in Iceland's historic wins over the Netherlands in EURO 2016 qualifying.

SKILLS

Great on the ball and with good awareness of the game, Sigurðsson creates chances for team-mates to score through his quick passing or he attempts to score himself, often via a long-range shot or one of his trademark lethal free-kicks.

MIDFIELDERS

THOMAS MÜLLER

COUNTRY: Germany
DATE OF BIRTH: 13.09.89
CLUB: Bayern Munich
CAPS: 68
GOALS: 31

PLAYER PROFILE
Bursting onto the scene as a youngster with Bayern, Müller shone at two FIFA World Cups and scored nine goals for Germany in qualifying for EURO 2016. A versatile footballer, he can play as a winger, central midfielder or at the front as a striker.

SKILLS
Müller finds space all over the pitch and frequently makes powerful runs into the opposing penalty area. Strong in the air and blessed with a powerful shot, he is a prolific scorer from midfield, with over 100 goals for club and country.

XHERDAN SHAQIRI

COUNTRY: Switzerland
DATE OF BIRTH: 10.10.91
CLUB: Stoke City
CAPS: 51
GOALS: 17

PLAYER PROFILE
Shaqiri made his debut for FC Basel in 2009 and then for Switzerland in 2010. He was named man of the match in each of his first two 2014 FIFA World Cup matches, and the following year he joined Stoke City from Internazionale for £12 million.

SKILLS
Quick-footed and playing mostly as a wide midfielder, Shaqiri beats opponents with his ball control and sudden changes of direction. He has a devastating shot, especially with his left foot, and notched up four goals and five assists in qualifying for EURO 2016.

LUKA MODRIĆ

COUNTRY: Croatia
DATE OF BIRTH: 09.09.85
CLUB: Real Madrid
CAPS: 87
GOALS: 10

PLAYER PROFILE
A four-time Croatian footballer of the year, Modrić was a linchpin in the Dinamo Zagreb team that won the 2007-08 Croatian First League by 28 points. A spell at Tottenham Hotspur followed, before he won the UEFA Champions League with Real Madrid in 2014.

SKILLS
Small and slight but deceptively strong, Modrić is a master passer of the ball and is adept at finding space. He can play in central midfield, linking play for team-mates, or a little further forward, providing crosses and assists or attempting to score himself.

DAVID SILVA

COUNTRY: Spain
DATE OF BIRTH: 08.01.86
CLUB: Manchester City
CAPS: 94
GOALS: 23

PLAYER PROFILE
Silva made his debut for Spain back in 2006. In 2010 he joined Manchester City, with whom he has won the English Premier League twice. EURO 2016 will be Silva's third UEFA European Football Championship. At the last, he was selected for the UEFA Team of the Tournament.

SKILLS
Silva may only be 1.7m tall, but he is a brilliant holder and passer of the ball. He is highly skilled at keeping possession for his team and fashioning goalscoring chances for team-mates or for himself.

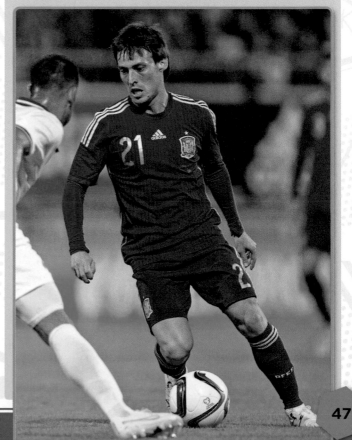

MIDFIELDERS

PAUL POGBA

COUNTRY: France
DATE OF BIRTH: 15.03.93
CLUB: Juventus
CAPS: 27
GOALS: 5

PLAYER PROFILE

Pogba debuted for France in 2013 and was named the FIFA World Cup Best Young Player the following year. Known as "Pogboom" for his explosive style, his drive and skills in midfield make him one of the most sought-after talents in Europe.

SKILLS

A fierce tackler, Pogba is comfortable playing the defensive midfielder role, shielding his defence and breaking up opposing attacks. He also loves to roam forwards at speed, breaking through the tightest defences with his spectacular shooting and skills on the ball.

BALÁZS DZSUDZSÁK

COUNTRY: Hungary
DATE OF BIRTH: 23.12.86
CLUB: Bursaspor
CAPS: 75
GOALS: 17

PLAYER PROFILE

The former Debrecen, PSV Eindhoven and Dinamo Moscow midfielder has won four league titles in the Netherlands and Hungary. In 2012, Dzsudzsák became Hungary's most expensive player after moving to Dinamo Moscow from Anzhi Makhachkala for around £13.8 million.

SKILLS

Operating mostly as a right winger, Dzsudzsák is capable of whipping telling crosses into the opposition's penalty area, or cutting inside to bear down on goal. He is also a threat from free-kicks.

MAREK HAMŠIK

COUNTRY: Slovakia
DATE OF BIRTH: 27.07.87
CLUB: Napoli
CAPS: 83
GOALS: 17

PLAYER PROFILE

Hamšik made his debut for Slovakia in 2007, the same year he moved to Napoli from Brescia. An attacking midfielder who can play deeper in midfield or out wide on the right, Hamšik's leadership has seen him captain both Napoli and Slovakia.

SKILLS

Hamšik can run with the ball under close control, but is especially skilled at passing, both short and long. He creates chances for team-mates to shoot, or scores himself, as his 13 goals and 12 assists for Napoli in the 2014-15 season show.

EDEN HAZARD

COUNTRY: Belgium
DATE OF BIRTH: 07.01.91
CLUB: Chelsea
CAPS: 63
GOALS: 12

PLAYER PROFILE

A winner of league titles in France with Lille and in England with Chelsea, Hazard is one of the most exciting attacking players in Europe, with over 100 goals in club football. He was voted the best player in the English Premier League for the 2014-15 season.

SKILLS

Quick and hard to mark, Hazard is brilliant at finding space to receive the ball, where his superb close control and dribbling allow him to run at defences. His vision and skill produce many assists for team-mates as well as goals for himself.

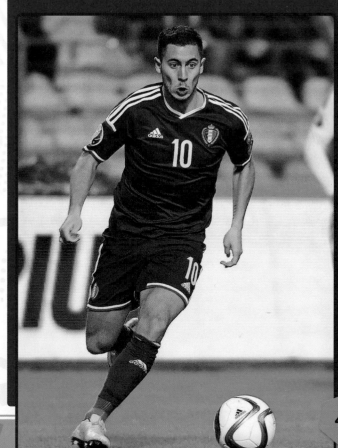

FORWARDS

OLIVIER GIROUD

COUNTRY: France
DATE OF BIRTH: 30.09.86
CLUB: Arsenal
CAPS: 44
GOALS: 13

PLAYER PROFILE
Giroud made his international debut for Les Bleus in 2011 and cemented his place in the national side with key goals in the 2014 FIFA World Cup qualifier against Spain before scoring his first FIFA World Cup goal against Switzerland.

SKILLS
At 1.92 metres tall, Giroud has a strong physical presence on the pitch and often has the edge in the air when it comes to headers. He's a fast mover, with the agility and strength to beat defenders and create goalscoring opportunities.

GARETH BALE

COUNTRY: Wales
DATE OF BIRTH: 16.07.89
CLUB: Real Madrid
CAPS: 54
GOALS: 19

PLAYER PROFILE
Bale was just 16 when he first appeared for Wales and has become his national team's talisman. His high-profile move from Tottenham Hotspur to Spanish giants Real Madrid saw him become Britain's most expensive footballer.

SKILLS
Incredibly fast and able to sprint the length of the pitch, Bale uses his pace and tall physique to pass opponents with ease. He can cross the ball with precision, strike powerful dipping or bending shots, and he frequently scores goals from free-kicks.

WAYNE ROONEY

COUNTRY: England
DATE OF BIRTH: 24.10.85
CLUB: Manchester United
CAPS: 109
GOALS: 51

PLAYER PROFILE
Rooney became England's youngest ever goalscorer aged 17 and has since won the English Premier League six times with Manchester United. He is England's captain and all-time top goalscorer, claiming the record with his 50th goal in September 2015.

SKILLS
One of England's most technically gifted players, Rooney has a powerful shot and can bend the ball. His stamina and determination see him pop up in unexpected places on the pitch. Physical, aggressive and, although not particularly tall, he is excellent in the air.

CRISTIANO RONALDO

COUNTRY: Portugal
DATE OF BIRTH: 05.02.85
CLUB: Real Madrid
CAPS: 123
GOALS: 55

PLAYER PROFILE
Ronaldo is a phenomenal footballer – one of the greatest players in the world. He's a star forward for both Real Madrid and Portugal, of which he is captain. Ronaldo has been selected for UEFA's Team of the Year for a record nine seasons.

SKILLS
One of the fastest players on the pitch, Ronaldo's speed and agility are matched by quick thinking and an array of stepovers and other tricks to beat opponents. A consistently top goalscorer with great drive, he's also a master at penalties and set pieces.

FORWARDS

ALEKSANDR KOKORIN

COUNTRY: Russia
DATE OF BIRTH: 19.03.91
CLUB: FC Dinamo Moscow
CAPS: 36
GOALS: 10

PLAYER PROFILE

A promising striker with EURO 2012 and 2014 FIFA World Cup experience, Kokorin has scored three goals during Russia's qualifying campaign and is considered one of the finest forwards in the Russian Premier League.

SKILLS

Hardworking and creative, Kokorin is a skilled passer of the ball, as well as an instinctive goalscorer. He is best known for his shooting, although he scored a powerful header from the edge of the penalty area in the 2014 FIFA World Cup.

MARIO MANDŽUKIĆ

COUNTRY: Croatia
DATE OF BIRTH: 21.05.86
CLUB: Juventus
CAPS: 63
GOALS: 20

PLAYER PROFILE

The first Croatian player to score in a UEFA Champions League final, Mandžukić has scored over 170 goals for clubs in Croatia, Germany, Spain and Italy, and has twice been Croatian footballer of the year (2012, 2013). He was joint top-scorer at EURO 2012.

SKILLS

Strong and able to run hard throughout a game, Mandžukić is a constant threat to opposing defenders, who he tries to drag out of position to create space for team-mates. A frequent goalscorer, he is powerful in the air and scores many headed goals.

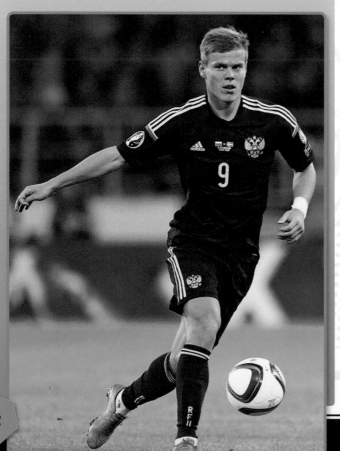

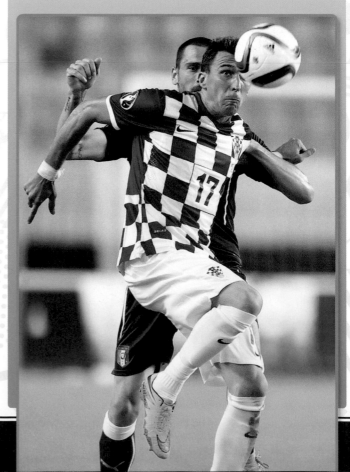

ANTHONY MARTIAL

COUNTRY: France
DATE OF BIRTH: 05.12.95
CLUB: Manchester United
CAPS: 6
GOALS: 0

PLAYER PROFILE

Martial became the world's most expensive teenage player in 2015 after his £36 million-move from AS Monaco to Manchester United, for whom he scored an explosive goal on his debut versus Liverpool. An exciting talent, he made his debut for the French national team in 2015.

SKILLS

Martial's greatest assets are his pace, lack of fear and natural eye for a goal. He strikes fierce shots on the run and uses his strength and speed to suddenly appear in goalscoring positions or to hound an opposition defence.

KYLE LAFFERTY

COUNTRY: Northern Ireland
DATE OF BIRTH: 16.09.87
CLUB: Norwich City
CAPS: 47
GOALS: 16

PLAYER PROFILE

After playing his club football throughout Europe, Lafferty spearheaded Northern Ireland's epic qualifying campaign. The Norwich City striker scored seven crucial goals and was man of the match in four out of the first five qualifying matches.

SKILLS

As a tall striker, Lafferty is very good in the air and a threat at corners and free-kicks. He is also deceptively quick and skilful on the ground, and is able to turn sharply to shoot or release a team-mate with a pass.

FORWARDS

ANDRIY YARMOLENKO

COUNTRY: Ukraine
DATE OF BIRTH: 23.10.89
CLUB: Dynamo Kyiv
CAPS: 55
GOALS: 22

PLAYER PROFILE

A two-time Ukrainian Premier League footballer of the year, Yarmolenko scored on his national team debut in 2009. His goal after 14 seconds versus Uruguay in 2011 was the fastest ever scored by a Ukrainian in an international game.

SKILLS

Tall and quick, Yarmolenko can cross, pass or shoot with both feet, making himself a goal threat from many positions on the pitch. He scored six times during Ukraine's EURO 2016 qualification campaign, often playing on the wing but sometimes as a second striker.

ROBERT LEWANDOWSKI

COUNTRY: Poland
DATE OF BIRTH: 21.08.88
CLUB: Bayern Munich
CAPS: 73
GOALS: 34

PLAYER PROFILE

Bayern Munich's Lewandowski is one of Europe's most feared strikers. He enjoyed an explosive start to 2015-16, scoring an incredible five goals in under nine minutes in a Bundesliga game and topping the scoring chart in EURO qualifying with 13 goals.

SKILLS

A goalscoring predator, Lewandowski uses short, sharp bursts of pace and acceleration to get free of defenders and into positions to unleash shots with either foot. He is a strong dribbler, works hard to chase down long balls, and helps out his defence too.

ZLATAN IBRAHIMOVIĆ

COUNTRY: Sweden
DATE OF BIRTH: 03.10.81
CLUB: Paris Saint-Germain
CAPS: 111
GOALS: 62

PLAYER PROFILE

The much-travelled maverick striker has scored more than 400 goals for club and country. He has won ten league titles in Italy, the Netherlands, Spain and most recently France, where in 2015 he became Paris Saint-Germain's all-time leading goalscorer.

SKILLS

Exciting and unpredictable, Ibrahimović has an eye for the unexpected, often scoring with thumping volleys off either foot, spectacular overhead kicks or agile headers. While not pacy, he can surprise and beat defenders with sudden turns or skilful ball control.

JON WALTERS

COUNTRY: Republic of Ireland
DATE OF BIRTH: 20.09.83
CLUB: Stoke City
CAPS: 38
GOALS: 10

PLAYER PROFILE

Walters made his international debut in 2010, the year that he moved to Stoke City and the English Premier League. He was a EURO play-off hero for the Republic in 2015, scoring twice to take his team to France.

SKILLS

Possessing great energy and stamina, Walters makes many attacking runs and tracks back to help out the defence. He is an attacking threat in the air, can hold the ball up well and is calm and composed when he gets a scoring chance in front of goal.

EURO RECORD BREAKERS

The 14 fantastic tournaments to date have yielded incredible action and performances, as well as a number of outstanding records. These include Michel Platini's record nine goals at the 1984 tournament and Spain's 4-0 win over Italy at UEFA EURO 2012 – the biggest margin of victory in a final.

Cristiano Ronaldo scored a hat-trick against Armenia in a June 2015 qualifier.

CLEAN-SHEET KEEPERS

The Netherlands' Edwin van der Sar (*below*) and Spain's Iker Casillas have both kept nine clean sheets at finals tournaments. At EURO 2012, Casillas let in only one goal, while van der Sar holds the record for the most game time at the EUROs – 1,535 minutes at four different finals tournaments.

TEAM TRIUMPHS

Germany have reached the EURO semi-finals a record eight times, progressing to the final on six occasions. Spain boast the longest gap between winning the tournament – on their debut in 1964 and then 44 years later in 2008. Portugal and the Czech Republic/Czechoslovakia have finished third or fourth the most times (three), while England hold the record for reaching the quarter-finals the most times (eight) without ever making it to the final.

RONALDO'S RECORDS

The youngest player to play in a EURO final is Cristiano Ronaldo. He was 19 years, 150 days old when he faced Greece at EURO 2004. Ronaldo has also scored the most goals, with 26 in qualifying and finals tournaments. The record for most goals in a single qualifying competition (13) is shared by Robert Lewandowski of Poland (EURO 2016 qualifying) and Northern Ireland's David Healy (EURO 2008 qualifying).

FIRST AND LAST

The fastest goal in a EURO finals game was scored in 2004 when Dmitri Kirichenko struck after just 68 seconds for Russia against Greece. By contrast, the latest goal was scored by Turkish striker Semih Şentürk against Croatia in the second minute of added time after 120 minutes of play. Şentürk's strike took the EURO 2008 quarter-final game into a penalty shoot-out, which Turkey won 3-1.

Turkey's Semih Şentürk celebrates his late goal in 2008.

COACHING SUCCESS

No coach has won the EUROs more than once. However, Joachim Löw (EURO 2008 and EURO 2012) and Berti Vogts (EURO '92 and EURO '96) have both led Germany for 11 games – the most for any coach. Löw (*right*) has the best record, winning eight matches, but Vogts' side were champions in 1996. Lars Lagerbäck is the only coach to have appeared at three EUROs in a row (2000, 2004 and 2008), managing Sweden on each occasion. He will be at EURO 2016 as Iceland's coach.

TOP-SCORING TEAMS AT THE EUROS

Year	Team	Goals
1960	Yugoslavia	6
1964	Hungary, Soviet Union, Spain	4
1968	Italy	3
1972	West Germany	5
1976	West Germany	6
1980	West Germany	6
1984	France	14
1988	Netherlands	8
1992	Germany	7
1996	Germany	10
2000	France, Netherlands	13
2004	England, Czech Republic	10
2008	Spain	12
2012	Spain	12

EURO 2016 PICTURE QUIZ

FLAG FINDER

Can you identify the right flag for each of these eight teams that will be competing at EURO 2016?

Albania
Russia
Belgium
Turkey

Iceland
Portugal
Spain
Croatia

1 2 3 4

1. _____
2. _____
3. _____
4. _____

5 6 7 8

5. _____
6. _____
7. _____
8. _____

GUESS WHO?

Three EURO 2016 superstars' heads are mixed up in this puzzle. Can you figure out who are they?

Greg
house
sterling

THE BIG MATCH

Can you match these 12 stars with the photos on page 59?
Write each name in the correct box.

Mesut Özil (Germany)
Yohan Cabaye (France)
Vincent Kompany (Belgium)
Jonny Evans (Northern Ireland)
Artem Dzyuba (Russia)
Mario Balotelli (Italy)

Zlatan Ibrahimović (Sweden)
Joe Hart (England)
Diego Costa (Spain)
Aaron Ramsey (Wales)
Tomáš Rosický (Czech Republic)
Kolbeinn Sigþórsson (Iceland)

HOW WELL DO YOU KNOW THE EUROS?

GREAT PLAYERS

1. Which player scored the most goals (9) in a single tournament and the fastest hat-trick at a UEFA European Football Championship?
a) Thomas Müller
b) Michel Platini
c) Cristiano Ronaldo

2. Which goalkeeper kept five clean sheets in a row at EURO 2012 (not including penalty shoot-outs)?
a) Manuel Neuer
b) Gianluigi Buffon
c) Iker Casillas

3. Which player has scored the most goals in UEFA European Football Championship qualifying and final tournaments, with 26 goals so far?
a) Wayne Rooney
b) Andrés Iniesta
c) Cristiano Ronaldo

4. Who is the only player to score two goals at three separate EURO finals tournaments?
a) Thierry Henry
b) Zlatan Ibrahimović
c) Jürgen Klinsmann

5. Against which team did Wayne Rooney (*right*) become England's all-time leading goalscorer during EURO 2016 qualifying?
a) Switzerland
b) San Marino
c) Estonia

MEMORABLE MOMENTS

1. Against which team did Spain's David Villa (*above left*) score a hat-trick at EURO 2008?
a) Italy
b) Russia
c) Sweden

2. Which team defeated France 5-4 to reach the final of the 1960 tournament?
a) Italy
b) West Germany
c) Yugoslavia

3. At EURO 2008, against which team were Turkey 2-0 down with 15 minutes to go, before winning the match 3-2?
a) Czech Republic
b) Netherlands
c) Croatia

4. Who was the first footballer to be shown a red card in the UEFA European Football Championship?
a) Alan Mullery (England)
b) Franco Baresi (Italy)
c) Franz Beckenbauer (West Germany)

5. Which tournament was the first to feature a penalty shoot-out in the final, won by Antonín Panenka's delicate chipped penalty?
a) 2004
b) 1992
c) 1976

TOP TEAMS

1. Which team were the only side to make their finals tournament debut at EURO 2012?
a) Ukraine
b) Turkey
c) Norway

2. Which is the only team to have reached the semi-finals three times and the final once, but never been champions?
a) Netherlands
b) Portugal
c) Sweden

3. Which team were the first (besides the hosts France) to qualify for EURO 2016?
a) Germany
b) Iceland
c) England

4. Which team recorded the largest ever victory in EURO qualification when they defeated San Marino 13-0 in 2006?
a) Spain
b) Netherlands
c) Germany

5. Which team did Greece beat twice at EURO 2004 on the way to becoming champions?
a) Germany
b) Portugal
c) Denmark

CHAMPIONS CHALLENGE

1. Which former country won the first UEFA European Football Championship in 1960?
a) Soviet Union
b) Yugoslavia
c) Czechoslovakia

2. Which country have been former champions, but have also lost the most EURO finals tournament games (14 in total)?
a) Denmark
b) France
c) Greece

3. Which team are the only side to have become champions twice, but not three times?
a) Italy
b) France
c) Spain

4. In 2012, which member of the champion side, Spain, was voted player of the tournament?
a) Xavi Hernandez
b) Fernando Torres
c) Andrés Iniesta

5. Which is the only EURO for which three-time champions Germany/West Germany attempted but failed to qualify?
a) 1968
b) 1980
c) 2004

TERRIFIC TOURNAMENTS

1. Which tournament featured Slavko and Slavek as mascots?
a) EURO 2008
b) EURO 2004
c) EURO 2012

2. Which team were the last hosts to reach the final of a EURO tournament?
a) Portugal (2004)
b) Netherlands (2000)
c) England (1996)

3. EURO 2000 featured the most goals scored at a finals tournament. What was the total?
a) 68
b) 73
c) 85

4. In which year was the UEFA European Football Championship first co-hosted by two countries?
a) 1992
b) 2000
c) 2008

5. At which tournament was a record average of 4.75 goals scored in every match?
a) 1976
b) 1988
c) 2004

61

GROUP A

10 June, 21.00	**France**	2	1	Romania	Saint-Denis
11 June, 15.00	**Albania**	0	1	Switzerland	Lens
15 June, 18.00	**Romania**	1	1	Switzerland	Paris
15 June, 21.00	**France**	2	0	Albania	Marseille
19 June, 21.00	**Switzerland**	0	0	France	Lille
19 June, 21.00	**Romania**	0	1	Albania	Lyon

TEAM	P	W	D	L	GD	Pts
France	3	2	1	0	4	7
Switzerland	3	1	2	0	2	6
Albania	3	1	1	1	1	3
Romania	3	0	1	2	2	1

GROUP B

11 June, 18.00	**Wales**	2	1	Slovakia	Bordeaux
11 June, 21.00	**England**	1	1	Russia	Marseille
15 June, 15.00	**Russia**	1	2	Slovakia	Lille
16 June, 15.00	**England**	2	1	Wales	Lens
20 June, 21.00	**Slovakia**	0	0	England	Saint-Étienne
20 June, 21.00	**Russia**	0	3	Wales	Toulouse

TEAM	P	W	D	L	GD	Pts
Wales	3	2	0	1	6	6
England	3	1	2	0	3	5
Slovakia	3	1	1	1	3	4
Russia	3	0	1	2	2	1

GROUP C

12 June, 18.00	**Poland**	1	0	Northern Ireland	Nice
12 June, 21.00	**Germany**	2	0	Ukraine	Lille
16 June, 18.00	**Ukraine**	0	2	Northern Ireland	Lyon
16 June, 21.00	**Germany**	0	0	Poland	Saint-Denis
21 June, 18.00	**N. Ireland**	0	1	Germany	Paris
21 June, 18.00	**Ukraine**	0	1	Poland	Marseille

TEAM	P	W	D	L	GD	Pts
Germany	3	2	1	0	3	7
Poland	3	2	1	0	2	7
N. Ireland	3	1	0	2	2	3
Ukraine	3	0	0	3	0	0

GROUP D

12 June, 15.00	**Turkey**	0	1	Croatia	Paris
13 June, 15.00	**Spain**	1	0	Czech Republic	Toulouse
17 June, 18.00	**Czech Rep.**	2	2	Croatia	Saint-Étienne
17 June, 21.00	**Spain**	3	0	Turkey	Nice
21 June, 21.00	**Croatia**			Spain	Bordeaux
21 June, 21.00	**Czech Rep.**			Turkey	Lens

TEAM	P	W	D	L	GD	Pts

GROUP E

13 June, 18.00	**Rep. Ireland**	1	1	Sweden	Saint-Denis
13 June, 21.00	**Belgium**	0	2	Italy	Lyon
17 June, 15.00	**Italy**	1	0	Sweden	Toulouse
18 June, 15.00	**Belgium**	3	0	Rep. Ireland	Bordeaux
22 June, 21.00	**Sweden**			Belgium	Nice
22 June, 21.00	**Italy**			Rep. Ireland	Lille

TEAM	P	W	D	L	GD	Pts

GROUP F

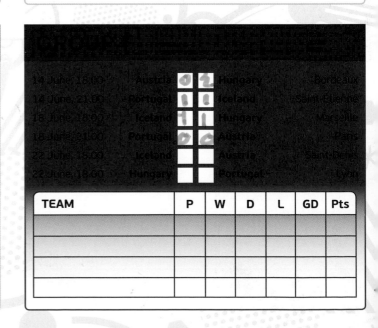

14 June, 18.00	**Austria**	0	2	Hungary	Bordeaux
14 June, 21.00	**Portugal**	1	1	Iceland	Saint-Étienne
18 June, 18.00	**Iceland**	1	1	Hungary	Marseille
18 June, 21.00	**Portugal**	0	0	Austria	Paris
22 June, 18.00	**Iceland**			Austria	Saint-Denis
22 June, 18.00	**Hungary**			Portugal	Lyon

TEAM	P	W	D	L	GD	Pts